Nobody Lives on Arthur Godfrey Boulevard

Books by Gerald Costanzo

Poetry

In the Aviary
The Laps of the Bridesmaids
Nobody Lives on Arthur Godfrey Boulevard

As Editor

Three Rivers: Ten Years
The Carnegie Mellon Anthology of Poetry

Limited Editions

Badlands
South Moccasin
Measuring the Tree
Wage the Improbable Happiness

Nobody Lives on Arthur Godfrey Boulevard

poems

Gerald Costanzo

BOA Editions, Ltd. / Brockport, NY, 14420 / 1992

ISBN: 0-918526-92-2 Cloth
ISBN: 0-918526-93-0 Paper

LC #: 92-72497

First Edition

Publications by BOA Editions, Ltd.
are made possible with the assistance of grants from the Literature Program of the New York State Council on the Arts and the Literature Program of the National Endowment for the Arts, as well as with financial assistance from private foundations, corporations, and individuals.

BOA Editions, Ltd. is a non-profit literary organization.

Cover Photo: James W. Hall
Cover Design: Daphne Poulin
BOA Logo: Mirko

Typesetting: ABC, Inc.
Manufacturing: McNaughton & Gunn, Lithographers

10 9 8 7 6 5 4 3 2 1

BOA Editions, Ltd.
A. Poulin, Jr., President
92 Park Avenue
Brockport, NY 14420

CONTENTS

IV The Man Who Invented Las Vegas

V Excavating the Ruins of Miami Beach

For my children

Lizabeth and Michael-James

I love America . . . . I love America so well that all its crudities and gross stupidities are no more to me than the little imperfections which give character and individuality to personal beauty. A windmill, a junk heap, and a Rotarian in their American setting have more meaning to me than Notre Dame, the Parthenon, or the heroes of the ages. I understand them. I get them emotionally. The stuff of this America which I know directly and immediately is to me more important actually and substantially than all the art of the past.

—Thomas Hart Benton

It is hard to laugh at the need for beauty and romance no matter how tasteless, even horrible, the results of that need are. But it is easy to sigh. Few things are sadder than the truly monstrous.

—Nathanael West
The Day of the Locust

Nobody Lives on Arthur Godfrey Boulevard

I

Dinosaurs of the Hollywood Delta

THE SACRED COWS OF LOS ANGELES

As if it had never happened
an old Angeleno will remember
the coming of the word *smog*.

How in 1948 a meteorologist
predicted the end of the past
in four letters. How the sacred

cows brought with them traffic
lights and street signs, cross-
walks and the dotted line,

which after a while they began
to ignore. Pausing at corners,
they'd drool a pool of oil

and maybe etch a rubber patch,
leaving. They were fed
whatever it took. They were washed

and shined. At night they'd idle
through La Cienega or watch
from a lovers' lane over

the cool Pacific. They'd snooze
beneath the flickering face
of the Escondido Drive-In

or sleep in garages, nestled
in the waning fumes—safe,
a few hours, from the future, safe

from the sight of the full moon,
a pomegranate resting
on the hazy lip of Los Angeles.

SNAKE

Because he lived
in one of those regions
where snake is the plural

of snake, when they told him
there were snake in his swamp
he understood. He did them in

with his shotgun. His daughter,
Magill, sometimes sobbed while
poling them out. The tears

in her eyes and the look in his:
a whole morning's religion—
and the corpse of snake

left be in the heat
not snake at all,
but several serpent.

INTRODUCTION OF THE SHOPPING CART

Oklahoma City, 1937

There was a man
who collected facts.

After work he rode twenty stories,
let himself in
to cartons filled with index cards
and his crucial lists.

Facts reveal useful lives.
He got things right.

The shopping cart invented
by Sylvan Goldman,
Oklahoma City, 1937.

When the man passed on
his relatives came.

P.T. Barnum had four daughters.

They searched through his cartons
for ten-dollar bills.

The sky, which on cloudless
days appears to be azure,
has no true color.

He wasn't eccentric.
When they found nothing,
they threw everything
out.

His final fact:
you live and you die.

The shopping cart. P.T. Barnum.

The sky.

HOUDINI DISAPPEARING IN PHILADELPHIA

Outside the theater
in his best bib and tucker,
we wondered where it was he went
once he'd reappeared.
Unlocked from that huge debris of chains
or risen from a trunk
bolted and submerged in a tank,
wouldn't he need a cold beer?

Wrists wringing with welts
as he held aloft the police handcuffs,
or loosed from a straight-jacket
night after night in fifty seconds flat,
maybe he needed to escape.

Most likely it was to a new woman,
one to whom he could finally
and without fear
confess it all.

The man who could get out
of anything.
He disappeared into a cab
and headed off up Broad Street's
well-lighted and imaginable breach.

NEWLYWED

The newlyweds
never watch closely

enough. The way the
preacher's appropriate

solemnity astounds them.
The way the best man

picks up the tab and slips
off into the receiving

line. There is something
to be said

for his rented
tuxedo, and the laps

of the bridesmaids are
no less luxurious.

The way the groom's
spinster sister sighs. The

way the guests, recognizing
an honorable intention

when they see one,
weep.

THE RESURRECTION OF LAKE ERIE

Everything before me turns to allegory
—Jose Emilio Pacheco

Soon after the word went out,
dismembered bodies cast off
in barrels by the mafiosi

fused, and hatching from those eggs
of slat, swam toward
the shore of the new life.

The rotting fish righted themselves
and went on. Plant life again.
And clear, warm breezes

moved through Cleveland, Dunkirk,
and Buffalo. In the air, geese,
their honking and a pleasure

in the sadness of natural life—
its second chance.
From the beaches the waving arms

of bathers signaled the freighters,
signaled the sloop cutting across
to Port Stanley.

DINOSAURS OF THE HOLLYWOOD DELTA

Joe DiMaggio, who was married for three years to
Marilyn Monroe, has ended a 20-year standing order
for thrice-weekly delivery of roses to her crypt.
The florist said Mr. DiMaggio gave no explanation.
—The New York Times
September 30, 1982

In times of plenty
they arrived from everywhere
to forage among the palmettos
of Beverly and Vine, to roam
the soda fountains and dime stores
of paradise. For every Miss Tupelo

who got a break, whose blonde
tresses made it to the silver screen,
whose studio sent her on a whirlwind
tour to Chicago, and to the Roxy
in Manhattan where she'd chat
with an audience, do a little tap

dance, and answer questions
about the morality of the jitterbug,
thousands became extinct.
Their beauty, it was said, drove
men to wallow in dark
booths in the Florentine

Lounge, dreaming of voluptuous
vanilla, though the rumor persists
that they were dumb.
They were called *Jean*, *Rita*, *Jayne*,
Mae, and *Betty*. The easy names.

No one remembers now
how the waning of their kind
began. Theories have pointed
to our own growing sophistication—
as if that were a part of natural
selection. At first we missed
them little, and only in that detached

manner one laments the passing
of any passing thing. Then posters
began to appear. Whole boutiques
adoring their fashion: heavy rouge,
thick lipstick. The sensuous puckering
of lips. Surreptitious giggling.

We began to congregate on street corners
at night, Santa Monica and La Brea,
to erect searchlights
and marquees announcing premieres
for which there were no films.
We looked upward

as if what had been taken from us
were somehow etched in starlight above
their sacred city. We began
to chant, demanding their return—
to learn, for once, the meaning
of their desperate, flagrant love.

II

Nobody Lives on Arthur Godfrey Boulevard

LIVING THE GOOD LIFE ON THE SAN ANDREAS FAULT

Every day in Daly City
is part of the beginning
of the end. There at the tip

where the great fault
runs from Mexico to lose
itself in the sea,

they wait for the one morning
when they will slide faster
than they do now

toward watery graves
beneath the Aleutians. How
the fiery night will extinguish

itself where the earth opens
to feed on its own tender
crust! For a hundred years

they will be the news
that diminishes slowly to
a simple lesson: *there is just*

cause for misgiving. Not all
our worry is needless.
This is the price they pay

for living the good life.
The price for the freedom
of extravagant loving, the food

and the cars. For the abundance
of mesmerization, the making it,
and the overlooked bountiful

losing. For the guilt. The price
they want to pay for living
in the midst of an enchantment

called America
which like every fairy tale
needs its wicked witch.

THE RIOT OF NICKEL BEER NIGHT

While the Red Sox were taking it
on the chin from the Twins,
and the Orioles were blowing
another big lead to the Yankees,
in the bottom of the ninth

in Cleveland some fan jumped
out of the stands and punched Jeff
Burroughs in the nose.
The customers in the right field
seats, not satisfied

by anything, not by the fireworks
and the smoke bombs,
not the ball game, not
by even this dream of three
hours with cheap beer, joined in.

For a bruiser like Burroughs
it was a defeat
he could stare in the face
and understand. He made
for the dugout as they flocked

after him. Afterwards the ump,
Nestor Chylak, forfeited it
to the Rangers. Nursing the bump
on his skull broached by an airborne
bottle, he told reporters

the fans stunk up the place—
the place was a zoo.
So it was no joke when, for days
after, the replay
from the center field camera

showed us those fans swarming
toward home plate like mobs of angry
birds inexplicably drawn
to the entrance
of a narrow tunnel

and, while the announcer
mumbled something about the modern
era, in the foreground the one
small boy,
sober and disinterested

in fisticuffs
but grateful for a chance
on the surface of the big time,
turning cartwheels across
the outfield.

MANHATTAN AS A LATIN-AMERICAN CAPITAL

How can this be happening in the Palace
of Justice? Senators,
Judges in their seasonal robes
fleeing through the burning colonnades!
Captains of industry escaping
in tinted limousines; the dictators
of fashion unheard from for weeks.
A Broadway of sawdust, dead poultry.
Guerrillas slowly metabolizing
the culture. Scattered resistance
in the Garment District. In the galleries
death squads, in the name of posterity,
machine-gunning, amigos,
all the precious art.

THE WHITE EXPERIENCE IN AMERICA

From the beginning
we were reared on the power
of illusion: Freedom:
Justice: Mannikins dressed
to resemble Hayley Mills

and Dean Jones
wrested from the fiery
train wrecks of the cinema.
Give us the Roseland Roller
Rink, the Tivoli, and the Acme

Arcade. The Brothers at Glastonbury
Abbey on any October morning
rising to pray. Drunks at the curb
in front of the bank on Vine
Street, where the men

with jackhammers are taking
a break. The diesel will save us.
The all-nite diner. Tell us
the truth about Jersey City
or Woonsocket and we will rage

in letters to the editor.
Remind us of witch hunts
and we will claim no credit
for the past, then admit
we have always been prepared

to give violence its chance.
Listen, what we've believed
is solid and manageable
like a thumbprint
or the College of Hard Knocks.

FATTY ARBUCKLE

Roscoe "Fatty" Arbuckle's career came to an abrupt end in 1921 after he was charged with manslaughter in the death of Virginia Rappe, a young starlet who was along for a Labor Day orgy he hosted in San Francisco.
—The Movie Book

The City Council of Minneapolis,
because of his crime of passion,
voted to ban him from their theaters.
When Paramount refused to release
his last picture in 1921, *that* America
received the news with great
indifference.

The alley is still there
down which a portly, disheveled
figure fled in the early hours.
The bedclothes had been dragged
from the two mattresses
and set afire at the head
of the stairs.

Fatty got his start at the age
of eight, appearing nightly
in black face with a stock
company in Kansas City.
At the end, forty-six, amid
rumors of more showgirls,
he died in his sleep.

People adored him
for *The Gangsters*, *Ben's Kid*,
and *Gasoline Gus*. One
of his ex-wives said he was always
an embarrassment: just an obese
uncle, beloved of millions,
a buffoon to those who knew him.

For a time he took the name
Will B. Good and became a director
in New York. That he was acquitted
after the third trial did
not matter.

Witnesses claimed Arbuckle came
out of the room— these depositions
of sexual conquest and its attendant
failure!— dressed in pajamas
and wearing Miss Rappe's Panama
hat cocked on the side of his head.
On his face, that fatuous grin.

NOBODY LIVES ON ARTHUR GODFREY BOULEVARD

When I first heard about America
it was already too late. When I learned
that its holiest city is Dallas,
Texas, there was nothing I could do
but bear witness to the deckled edge

of manifest destiny, California
well on its way to becoming
an island, or some foreign country
where one of the many forms
of English is still spoken.

I had missed the arduous construction
of democracy, though I lived among
its numbered days. What I saw
was the Reconstruction of Fifth Avenue,
and the Army Corps of Engineers

dredging sand from the sea
and piling it back where the beaches
belong. I heard wry assemblages
of Rotarians, Shriners, and Optimists,
Elks and Moose committing business

over lunch. I listened as
my friends wondered at the poverty
which affluence breeds,
not quite believing in the life
lived on Frank Sinatra Drive,

nor in the one where nobody lives
on Arthur Godfrey Boulevard. I watched
brotherhood practiced among corporations,
and freedom in the emporiums
of fast food. The separation of church

and religion. I saw all of us
becoming stranded everywhere
in our land, the new Pilgrims arrived
at last on the shore of a great
desert, mouthing our own sad psalms.

III

The Rise of the Sunday School Movement

BRAILLE

The blind folding their dollar
bills in half. Giving the fives
a crease on each corner; leaving
the tens smooth as a knuckle.

There are ways, even in trust
among the rank and file
of the seeing,
not to be bilked.

The blind leading the blind
is not so bad—

how it is lost on us every day
that you can learn all
of the world you need to know
by tapping it gently
with a stick.

JUNGLES

If nothing between you
and this world was right,
you never said as much.

One day, without leaving,
you simply retreated to
seek your fortune

as if some California still
existed, as if it were a state
of mind. You learned

the rootlessness within
the body makes that journey
difficult.

Those letters to your
loved one in Pennsylvania
from whichever remote

village inside yourself
you sent them
told her of nothing but your

exquisite and declining
penmanship. Years later,
informed of your death,

I think of all the time
we spend probing the dark
continents of ourselves,

of what happens when a man
at last, unshaven and ill-kempt,
walks out of the jungles

of his own heart
carrying not even so much
as an answer.

THE MAJESTIC

They built it
as an evangelical
temple, and on its roof

the members of an obscure
sect waited for a signal
to ascend into heaven.

When it became a theater,
various Little Evas
simulated that ascent

on cue seven
nights a week. The windows
are grimy with smoke

now, the roof nearly gone.
The seasons, for those
who love the seasons,

still pass, from burlesque
to drama to vaudeville,
specter of the garish banners

billing the 'farcical,'
the 'shapely,' the 'comical,'
and the 'raucous'—

their million stories,
real or imagined, reduced
to just this *one*.

SEEING MY NAME IN TV GUIDE

It was there, early Sunday
morning, in the Seattle Edition.
I was the writer on the arts

program reading selections
from his recent book,
opposite a wild party causes

a teen-age girl to question her
values, a run-in with the school
principal teaches Davey

that God is approachable, and Ronald
Reagan in good form as an ex-marshal
who has to clean up a lawless town

before he can settle down.
In the next hour *Insight* focussed
on the National Conscience,

Uncle Joe fell for a visiting
librarian, Tippi Hedren
discussed her pets.

THE OLD NEIGHBORHOOD

There was a time in my life when,
each evening after work,
I'd go down and sit in the bowling
alley. It was the only place

I could feel superior then,
watching the men in their leisure
suits and the funny shoes,
their fluffy-honey wives in toreadors

who always needed a few more
pointers just to get it wrong again.
I began to learn the strange
power that comes of watching well:

I knew the exhilaration in a mounting
score for Flo's Boutique or Genuine
Auto Parts. I wanted for myself
these simple feats destined

to be the life of the next beer-
blast. I began to want something
funny to tell the guys down
at some plant—

instead of only the wondering
at how things happen, at how
people I loved and people I didn't
crept up on me even while

I was paying attention,
at how I'd come to be sitting
night after night
between the soda fountain

and the scorers' benches,
unwelcome in the old
neighborhood
once more.

WASHINGTON PARK

I went walking in the Rose Gardens.
It was about to rain, but the roses
were beginning to bloom. The Olympiads,

some Shreveports, and the Royal
Sunsets. This was in the beautiful
city I had taken away from myself

years before, and now I was giving it back.
I walked over the Rosaria tiles
and found Queen Joan of 1945. I sat

on the hillside overlooking the reservoir
and studied the Willamette and the Douglas
firs. I learned the traffic

and the new highrises as the rain
came down.
                    This leaving and returning,

years of anger and forgiveness,
the attempts to forgive one's self—
it's everybody's story,

and I was sitting there
filling up again with the part of it
that was mine.

THE RISE OF THE SUNDAY SCHOOL MOVEMENT

"I am not a healer. Jesus is the healer.
I am only the little girl who opens the door
and says 'Come in'."
—Aimee Semple McPherson

I had wanted my daughter
to become an evangelist—
Sister Lizabeth Adrienne, say—
not to relive my life in hers,
nor for desire after the great abstraction

in lieu of the bits of carpentry
I've managed. No, like anyone
I just longed for a little pomp amid
all of this circumstance.
A progeny who could shout *Sweet*

Beautiful Jesus and mean it.
To have borne
a pillar in the rise
of the Sunday School Movement,
or one of the overdue

Northern Crusades. One who could
espy the dance halls of Venice,
California, with the true conviction
of a Sunday afternoon; who could bathe
in the sea at Carmel and not

disappear for three weeks
in Mexico with her married lover;
who'd never be transported
back from the lost, paraded
in a throne of white

wicker from her private train car
to overdose on tablets
of the newest redemption.
The way I figured it,
I'd be sitting at a corner table

in the Desdemona Club
nursing a brew. She'd be up
there on the large-screen TV next
to the bar, having taken over Billy
Graham's Asian Tour after his terrible

swift heart attack in China. The petite
brunette beauty from America!
She'd be singing *Lord,*
We Need Thee Every Hour as
the afflicted clutched at the hem

of her flowing dress. Maybe
I'd kneel among them, then
and there. Begin
to believe as we're able to believe
what reaches us by satellite—

bow down as she gave us
the beauteous word, all of us praising,
loving her, adoring the celestial
melody, possessed by our irrevocable
conversions.

IV

The Man Who Invented Las Vegas

LANDSCAPE WITH UNEMPLOYED JOCKEYS

It was a landscape
with unemployed jockeys,
a landscape of rubric
and confection.
One could imagine
the outskirts of Louisville
and from there, who knows?—
the fringes of Tulsa
and on along the power
lines to Blanche Laborde, Queen
of Long Beach, crooning
Love Me With All Your Heart;
the theatrics of Darius
Lawrence or Bertha
Lammell. It was a landscape
wherein the boots
were spiffed and shined,
and the riding breeches held up
with suspenders. A landscape
of dejection and fluency,
of idle tack.
It was a landscape
with unemployed jockeys,
the colors of their silks
dazzling and littering
the hillsides and nothing
doing at the downs.

STARGAZERS

in memory of Frank Stanford

Whoever predicted the silver Cadillac
parked in the lot,
that fez of an American
potentate left behind on the seat,
whoever diverted words
like *mercurial* into the horoscopes
and foretold croupiers bent
over gaming tables
in the half-light, offering
the beginning of religion again,
whoever felt the constant movement
of even the furthest stars
as they bruise the air we breathe
could decipher a farmer
standing deep in his field
swatting the flies from his face,
the press-agent visiting his daughter
in Des Moines,
or *a fat lady in a housecoat*
walking through rooms with a cage,
calling a bird.

JEANE DIXON'S AMERICA

San Francisco remains in grave personal
danger. Dubuque continues to be a source
of consternation for the entire Hawkeye
state. Tensions could diminish, though only
through an act of subterfuge.

New Jersey will be named in a paternity
suit, but will wage battle in open
court to preserve its good name.
Look for Minneapolis and St. Paul
to split, this time for good. Each
will agree they were never meant
to be together.

New York City will embark on a religious
pilgrimage, either to Rome or Jerusalem.
But there can be no forgiveness.
Overnight stardom is putting a great deal
of pressure on Missoula, Montana, which will
have to choose its roles carefully
in the coming months or risk
being a ghost town by the end of the decade.

Peoria must keep itself from overexposure
once again this year. If it succeeds, its
many problems will continue to go unnoticed.
Honolulu, weary of the long commute,
longs to be part of the mainland,
especially of southern California.
But with things the way they are now,
don't look for this to happen
any time soon.

CARL YASTRZEMSKI

Harwich, Massachusetts 1981

When the bratty kids
followed me out of the ballpark
demanding my autograph,
I told them they had the wrong guy.

Yaz lived in our summer
town, while his college boy played
for the local team. He'd been seen
seldom and so, like every hero,
remained larger than life but smaller
than rumor. These ruffians
wanted his signature and what
could I do in the minute I wasn't *him*
and only I knew it.

When they grabbed
at my windbreaker and went
for my Bosox cap, I sprinted
through the parking lot
and into the car just as Yaz
must have done that first time
he'd driven off, heart pounding,
a real American night the diminishing
radius of his anonymity.

At home,
my wife and children asleep,
everything locked up, I sat in the low
light of the study. Oh, I'd played ball
in my day alright. Whiffed against
Little Leaguers who later made the Majors,
who in our 29th year were referred
to as "veterans" while I received lesser
acclaim for being young at what I do.

As sometimes happens,
I began to write it down.
Not this, but something like it
about falling beneath a knockdown pitch
just in time. Getting up and digging in,
and busting a high hard one out of sight
when maybe the real story was just
a misunderstanding with the boss
or an article in the *Times* about Frankie
Lymon's widows.

I did this night after night
with the dedication of Yaz
and the consolation of nobody wanting
the real me to sign anything. Alone,
tapping the plate before thousands of fans,
swinging for the fences with the childhood
of Johnny Carson or a television memory
of the Dalai Lama. Stroking line drives
with nothing in my hands but Aristophanes
on *the bitterness of figs.*

Year after
year, with no Ford dealership
for the off season, without a big contract
or hope for arbitration. Over
and over I'd do it, not for the fame,
god, not for the money,
but for what darker, sweeter
compensation?

POEM FOR THE INTERCHANGING OF OUR SENSES

Camels have been used by man as a beast of burden
for many years, which may be why they seem to detest
human beings.

—sign in the Portland, Oregon Zoo

I have come to exchange
the eyes of the camel

for the eyes of
the whale,

not only to understand salt
and endurance.

                    To trade
the obsidian eyes

of rodents
for the dead-eyes of hawks.

I've come to exchange
the slow eye of the hurricane

for the tireless eye
of the elephant

                    not just,
with the memory of persistent

boredom, to learn absence
in the midst of fury.

I'm going to exchange
the eyes of Marilyn

Monroe for the eyes of Mother
Teresa,

                    the stare of Mike
Tyson with the stare

of Einstein.
I have come wanting to see

the world in a way
other than the way I see it.

Wanting all of us
to see and to hear it differently.

                      The eyes
of Stalin

for the eyes of Walt Disney,
not solely to witness

armies of animated
dogs, dwarves and mice

with full complements
of actual artillery

                         march off
to wage the improbable

happiness. I'd like to
be able to say to myself

now you know
the generations and the pressures

it took
for Pennsylvania to crush

your bones
into coal. Now you know

all the sounds
of Napoleon's arrogance,

the true rolling of Eddie
Cantor's eyes as he

awoke from a nightmare,
Tolstoy listening to the serfs,

and now you know
how Edison felt

when his angered mother
boxed his ears.

THE MAN WHO INVENTED LAS VEGAS

In church he never felt
the weight of God which hangs
in those places heavier

than any mist; he felt only
the overwhelming presence of
luck. When he knelt, his bones

cracked like loaded dice
and fell into place. The choirs
he heard were of roulette wheels

spinning in rooms velvet
and vacant of light as an altar
without candles. He saw

middle-aged housewives
grown tired of marriages more
sour than lemons standing in rows,

pulling the levers of slot
machines again and again, often
not seeing the final combinations

of their unexotic fruit. The
fascinations of boredom and
chance! He gathered electricity

and with its flashes and spurts
and steady rays turned darkness
out of the desert forever,

thinking *we shall never sleep*.
He witnessed the spectacle
from a distance, and in

the trance of a child staring
into his first fire,
learning the beauty and heat

of its rage. And he thought not
that it was good or bad,
but that what he had made

was a thing some of the people
who live on earth for a while
could believe in.

V

Excavating the Ruins of Miami Beach

BOURNEHURST-ON-THE-CANAL

They arrive in the blustery
summer twilight, couples in coupes,
roadsters and touring cars, up

from Falmouth and Hyannisport
in Palm Beach suits and taffeta weave.
There is dancing to Paul Whiteman

and Alice Fay. What summons
our attention— my mother-in-law told
me this— is not the soft flags luffing

at each high corner of the pavilion,
nor the placards for photoplays screened
—during the week and after the season—

on the lower level. Not the darkened
interior, the bandstand surrounded
by potted ferns and huge portal

archways, those boxed lights
with dim figures of dancing goddesses
suspended from the iron

mesh ceiling. Never mind
that all of this will burn to the cliffside
in the autumn of 1933. Tonight it is

the one couple, vaguely familiar, lingering
by the path. They are having a quarrel—
over sex or money, because what else

could it be? Never mind that within thirty
years their eldest daughter will be
a school marm in another part

of the state; that their youngest,
surely the more beautiful and promising,
will have entered into an arrangement

with the Rathbone sisters
which will be marked by sadness
and disappointment. Never mind that their

only son, a graduate of Colby College,
will live in Cleveland and embark
on a livelihood seldom

mentioned at family gatherings. Tonight
they are young, and are having
a quarrel. It is one of those evenings

full of such stirrings as only memory
will adequately "take into account." Just now
the orchestra strikes up and music

floats over the distance to where they are
being a little brusque with each other,
a little stubborn.

And now, as if called, they begin to move
toward the ballroom entrance, he slightly ahead
and tugging at her wrist, though not quite

so much to cause pain.
He believes the moment has passed
and he is leading her toward

an evening of happiness.
Toward a lifetime
of happiness.

THE STORY

For years I tried
to write the story called
"Excavating the Ruins of Miami
Beach." I guess I needed
to give some meaning
to that time after the divorce
when my life, all alcohol
and remorse, moved at a pace
far slower than I could adapt
to; one of those times when living
becomes a cruel parody
of our intention.

After ten months,
we were back together—
for who knows what reasons.
We could not live with each other,
then couldn't successfully
live apart. Still there was bitterness.
The accusations. Even deceit. Everything
wreckage and impossibility.

It was the summer we took
our children on that loopy
odyssey across the South
just to avoid the place where trouble
was—at least the part of it
that wasn't us. I think now
we were lucky to live in a country
where you can become someone
else so easily.

* * *

At the south end of Miami Beach,
just off Collins Ave., beyond
the beautiful seedy tropical Deco hotels
and beside the Adler Burlesque,
years out of its time, the sidewalk
sandwich-board proclaiming *Songstress*
Claire Barry of the Famous 'Barry Sisters'
and Hilarious Comedian Larry Best
with his Apple Routine— Next Week:
the Vibrant Voice of the Lovely Helen
Marr, was a lunch counter named Big
Daddy's. I walked in,
my four-year-old son on my hand,
and there were the photographs
that made the minute-to-minute
I was living seem less immediate, less
full of consequence, again.
On the walls hundreds of group portraits
of the proprietor and his family alongside
celebrities, all their names stamped out
in tape-gun plastic and affixed
to the frames: Big Daddy, Mrs. Big Daddy,
and the kid— Big Daddy Jr., posed among
Tiny Tim, Johnny Weismuller, Henny
Youngman, Roland LaStarza, Troy
Donohue, and Dr. Joyce Brothers.

My son at his meal, I roved
the mystical gallery: Myron Cohen, Fabian,
Jack E. Leonard, Frank Sinatra Jr.,
Patty Duke, and Jose Ferrer. I remember
dreaming, in this land of lunch hour
patrons and the adult incarnation
of Big Daddy Jr. teaching two Vietnamese
boys to wipe down a table, that I
was an archaeologist. I remember laughing.

* * *

I couldn't write
the story, though I lived in it
for a while and was myself
occupied.
                    Walking out, my son
eager for his own next episode,
I understood from the curious half-hour
that— hard as I tried— I couldn't solve
any of my problems; and that this,
finally, was how I'd begun
to outgrow them.

EXCAVATING THE RUINS OF MIAMI BEACH

After months of drilling
and digging, of carving out
the central trench,

they had come down
through layers of soil and cement,
through sand rife with shells—

ample debris of a Cenozoic sea-bed—
to arrive at the entrance
of a narrow hollow. A phalanx

entering the darkness,
they were astonished, as they lowered
themselves beneath the rotted

ceiling timbers, at the reflections
their lights gave back
of objects fastened to the walls.

Ancient pictographs—
all the artifacts one could covet
in a findspot. The names

had been affixed
in an archaic plastic script,
decipherable in shallow

embossing: Big Daddy and Dr. Erwin
Stillman; Big Daddy and Patty Duke.
This in the midst of something

called a Hot Dog Stand
in the fallen United States. Big
Daddy and Shecky Greene.

Here was the patriarch
in a thousand proofs, his Little
Mama with her buxom personality.

They began to dust and wash
the relics of this fossil beach,
to preserve something

of their own history. Big Daddy
and Norm Crosby. Big Daddy
and Totie Fields and Jerry Vale.

And since this was *all* they knew—
all this much—
they assumed they knew it all.

ACKNOWLEDGMENTS

Grateful acknowledgment is made to editors of the following periodicals in which these poems, some in slightly different form, first appeared:

Carolina Quarterly: "Jungles"
Epoch: "Newlywed" (as "Marriage Dealers")
The Georgia Review: "Nobody Lives on Arthur Godfrey Boulevard"
Gulfstream: "The Story" and "Excavating the Ruins of Miami Beach"
Kansas Quarterly: "Dinosaurs of the Hollywood Delta"
Memphis State Review: "Living the Good Life on the San Andreas Fault"
MidAtlantic Review: "Poem for the Interchanging of Our Senses"
The Missouri Review: "Braille" and "Stargazers"
North American Review: "The Sacred Cows of Los Angeles," "Jeane Dixon's America," and "The Rise of the Sunday School Movement"
North Dakota Quarterly: "Manhattan as a Latin-American Capital," "Landscape with Unemployed Jockeys," and "Seeing My Name in *TV Guide*"
The Oconee Review: "The Old Neighborhood"
The Ohio Review: "The Resurrection of Lake Erie," "Introduction of the Shopping Cart," and "Snake"
Ploughshares: "Bournehurst-on-the-Canal"
Poetry Now: "The Riot of Nickel Beer Night" and "Houdini Disappearing in Philadelphia"
Prairie Schooner: "Washington Park"
Raccoon: "The Majestic"
The Reaper: "The White Experience in America"
The Sole Proprietor: "The Man Who Invented Las Vegas"
Willow Springs: "Carl Yastrzemski" and "Fatty Arbuckle"

"Braille" appeared in the *1981 Anthology of Magazine Verse and Yearbook of American Poetry*, edited by Alan F. Pater (Monitor Books); "Dinosaurs of the Hollywood Delta" appeared in *The Pushcart Prize X: Best of the Small Presses*, edited by Bill Henderson (Pushcart Press/Viking-Penguin) and in the *1985 Anthology of Magazine Verse and Yearbook of American Poetry;* "The Rise of the Sunday School Movement" appeared in *The Pushcart Prize XII: Best of the Small Presses;* "Nobody Lives on Arthur Godfrey Boulevard," "Jeane Dixon's America," and "Introduction of the Shopping Cart" appeared in *The Morrow Anthology of Younger American Poets*, edited by Dave Smith and David Bottoms (William Morrow and Company); "Seeing My Name in *TV Guide*" appeared in *Light Year 1988-89*, edited by Robert Wallace (Bits Press); "The Sacred Cows of Los Angeles" appeared in *Gridlock: An Anthology of Poetry About Southern California*, edited by Elliott Fried (Applezaba Press), and in*Traveling America with Today's Poets*, edited by David Kherdian (Macmillan); and "Dinosaurs of the Hollywood Delta" and "Excavating the Ruins of Miami Beach" appeared in *Decade Dance: A Celebration of Poems*, edited by Mark Sanders (Sandhills Press).

Some of these poems were published in a fine press, limited edition collection, *Wage the Improbable Happiness*, by Bits Press, Cleveland, 1982.

The author wishes to express his gratitude to the National Endowment for the Arts for Creative Writing Fellowships during which time the poems in this collection were begun, and later, for time in which the work was revised and completed; and to the Pennsylvania Council on the Arts for an Individual Fellowship award. Special thanks to Peter Carnahan for his counsel and support over the past dozen years.

Thanks are due as well to Carnegie Mellon University for two President's Fund for the Humanities Grants.

Some of these poems, when first published in magazines, carried the following dedications which I wish to acknowledge here:

"The Old Neighborhood" is for Gerald Stern; "Snake" for Susan Petrie McLaughry; "Jeane Dixon's America" for Jim Crumley; "The Resurrection of Lake Erie" for William Boggs; "Landscape with Unemployed Jockeys" for Allyson Hunter; "Washington Park" for Grace McGinnis; and "Manhattan as a Latin-American Capital" for Sally Cortese and Annamae Lawson.

Gerald Costanzo

Gerald Costanzo was born in Portland, Oregon, in 1945. He is editor of *Three Rivers Poetry Journal* and the Carnegie Mellon University Press Poetry Series. A graduate of Harvard, and of The Writing Seminars at Johns Hopkins, his collections of poems include *In the Aviary* (winner of the Devins Award), and *The Laps of the Bridesmaids*. He has received two Creative Writing Fellowships from the National Endowment for the Arts as well as awards from the Pennsylvania Council on the Arts and the Coordinating Council of Literary Magazines. He lives in Harwich, Massachusetts, and near Pittsburgh, Pennsylvania, where he is Professor of English at Carnegie Mellon University.

BOA Editions, Ltd.
American Poets Continuum Series

Vol.	1	*The Führer Bunker:* *A Cycle of Poems in Progress* W. D. Snodgrass
Vol.	2	*She* M. L. Rosenthal
Vol.	3	*Living With Distance* Ralph J. Mills, Jr.
Vol.	4	*Not Just Any Death* Michael Waters
Vol.	5	*That Was Then:* *New and Selected Poems* Isabella Gardner
Vol.	6	*Things That Happen* *Where There Aren't Any People* William Stafford
Vol.	7	*The Bridge of Change:* *Poems 1974–1980* John Logan
Vol.	8	*Signatures* Joseph Stroud
Vol.	9	*People Live Here:* *Selected Poems 1949–1983* Louis Simpson
Vol.	10	*Yin* Carolyn Kizer
Vol.	11	*Duhamel:* *Ideas of Order in Little Canada* Bill Tremblay
Vol.	12	*Seeing It Was So* Anthony Piccione
Vol.	13	*Hyam Plutzik: The Collected Poems*
Vol.	14	*Good Woman:* *Poems and a Memoir 1969–1980* Lucille Clifton
Vol.	15	*Next: New Poems* Lucille Clifton
Vol.	16	*Roxa: Voices of the Culver Family* William B. Patrick
Vol.	17	*John Logan: The Collected Poems*
Vol.	18	*Isabella Gardner: The Collected Poems*
Vol.	19	*The Sunken Lightship* Peter Makuck

Vol.	20	*The City in Which I Love You* Li-Young Lee
Vol.	21	*Quilting: Poems 1987–1990* Lucille Clifton
Vol.	22	*John Logan: The Collected Fiction*
Vol.	23	*Shenandoah and Other Verse Plays* Delmore Schwartz
Vol.	24	*Nobody Lives on Arthur Godfrey Boulevard* Gerald Costanzo